Trusting the Mind

信
心
銘

Zen Epigrams

by Seng Ts'an

translated by Red Pine

Published by Empty Bowl Press
14172 Madrona Drive
Anacortes, Washington 98221
emptybowl.org

Printed by McNaughton & Gunn
960 Woodland Drive East
Saline, Michigan 48176

ISBN 978-0-912887-81-4

Photos by Bill Porter:
Third Patriarch Temple and Seng-ts'an Stupa

Cover and interior design by Tonya Namura
using Minion Pro

For Silas Hoadley

Translator's Preface

This is a book of epigrams, epigrams that encapsulate the teaching the Buddha first transmitted 2,400 years ago when he held up a flower and Kashyapa smiled. They're that simple. The Chinese call them *ming* 銘. Like the epigrams of ancient Greece, they consist of couplets that can stand alone or be linked together. And like their Mediterranean counterparts, they were inscribed, rather than spoken or sung. They were embroidered, carved, or written on all sorts of things: doorways, tombstones, ritual bronzes, even items of daily use like washbasins and writing brushes. Their salient feature was a few pithy phrases conveying something worth keeping in mind, and they usually rhymed. For example, taxes in ancient China were paid in silk, and this epigram was embroidered on robes: "The silkworms suffered / the weaving women weren't pleased / any new taxes / we're all sure to freeze." 桑蠶苦，女工難，得新捐，故後必寒. Ezra Pound took his motto from one inscribed on the washbasin of a king who lived 4,000 years ago: "Make it new / new every day / and make it new again." 苟日新，日日新，又日新.

Despite its antiquity and widespread use, the *ming* never played an important role among China's literary forms. Simply put, its diction was that of a Hallmark card. Most of those that have survived haven't survived because of their content but because of their connection with their author or the objects on which they were inscribed. The ones in this poem are an exception.

Among the tens of thousands that have been recorded, these are the only ones people still read and ponder. They're an essential part of Zen instruction around the world. Not only are they short and sweet, they're a good example of how a teaching that eschews the use of language to convey its message uses language.

Their author was a Chinese Buddhist monk named Seng-ts'an 僧璨 (pinyin: Sengcan). We know so little about him, some doubt he existed. But since a likely story is better than no story at all, I've put together the following account from the earliest records in which he appears, including the Hsukaosengchuan 續高僧傳 (c. 660) and the Litaifapaochi 厲代法寶記 (774).

Our enigma first shows up in 552 when he became a disciple of Hui-k'o 慧可, Zen's Second Patriarch. He was over forty, and it was Hui-k'o who gave him the name Seng-ts'an, meaning "Jewel among Monks." Hui-k'o was living north of the Yellow River at this time near the Northern Ch'i 北齊 capital of Yeh 鄴, or modern Handan 邯鄲.

Twenty-five years later, there was a change of dynasties. The Northern Ch'i was replaced by the Northern Chou 北周, and the new government decided it needed to expand its tax base. It began by forcing hitherto tax-exempt monks and nuns to return to lay life or be killed. Hui-k'o fled south to the remote slopes of Ssukungshan 司空山, just north of the Yangtze. Among those who accompanied him was Seng-ts'an.

The persecution of Buddhist clerics ended with the founding of the Sui dynasty 隋代 in 581, and Hui-k'o eventually returned north. But before he did, he designated Seng-ts'an as his Dharma heir, making him the Third Patriarch of Zen. That was in 583. After his teacher's departure, Seng-ts'an remained on Ssukungshan. But while the mountain was a good place to hide, it wasn't a good place to teach. Even today it sees few visitors. In 590 he finally ended his seclusion and took up residence at Shankussu 山谷寺 (Mountain Gorge Temple). It was only a few days walk away, and it was at the foot of Tienchushan 天柱山. Tienchushan was a sacred mountain, and it saw a constant stream of pilgrims. It should have been a good place to teach. But it was a Taoist mountain, and Seng-ts'an only attracted one disciple that we know of: a twelve-year-old boy who showed up at the monastery in 592.

Seng-ts'an gave the boy the name Tao-hsin 道信, "Tao Truster." Ten years later, in 601, Seng-ts'an made him his Dharma heir and Zen's Fourth Patriarch then left with some Taoist friends for the distant mountain of Lofushan 羅浮山, not far from what is now Hong Kong. Living near Tienchushan, Seng-ts'an had developed an interest in more than Taoist terminology. He suffered from rheumatism, and no place was more famous for elixirs than Lofushan.

By the time he returned two years later, Tao-hsin had left on his own peripatetic journey—a journey that would result in the establishment of China's first Zen monastery and the self-supporting communal way of life that would form the basis of what became Chinese Zen.

Despite the elixirs, Seng-ts'an died at Shanku Temple in 606, three years after he got back. His body was at first preserved. People in those days thought the preserved bodies of spiritual teachers had magic powers. Eventually, the magic wore out, and his body was cremated in 745 and the ashes placed inside a stupa. A number of prominent monks, including the Tientai master Chan-jan 湛然 (711-782), petitioned Emperor Su-tsung 肅宗 to honor Seng-ts'an, and the emperor agreed. In 761, he ordered Shanku Monastery renamed "Third Patriarch Temple." The temple is still there, and so is the stupa, on top of the hill behind the original monastery. Inscribed on its base is the Hsinhsinming 信心銘, the poem that has been associated with Seng-ts'an ever since.

As to when he wrote it, or how it found its way into the world, is anyone's guess. The dissemination of texts in those days depended on oral recitation or copying by hand. It's a wonder his poem made it beyond the monastery gate. But it did. Perhaps he handed out copies to pilgrims on their way up Tienchushan, or perhaps his Dharma heir, Tao-hsin, shared it with his disciples.

Lately some scholars have wondered if Seng-ts'an was really the author, or if it wasn't written by someone else. They have noted that Seng-ts'an was not listed as the author of the Hsinhsinming until his name was attached to the text in the Transmission of the Lamp 景德傳燈錄, published shortly after 1004. The same scholars have also noted similarities of the Hsinhsinming with another set of Zen epigrams titled Hsinming 心銘, written by a Zen master named Niu-t'ou Fa-jung 牛頭法融 (594-657). And some have gone so far as to suggest that it was Fa-jung who was the author of the Hsinhsinming, not Seng-ts'an.

Faced with such a possibility, I compared both texts. By the time I was done, I couldn't help wonder how anyone could link the authorship of something as simple and relentless as the Hsinhsinming with something as dense and rambling as the Hsinming. But maybe that's just me.[6] In the end, we have this text, regardless of who wrote it, and it might be just the thing for someone looking for an epigram or two.

I considered translating it half a dozen times. The language is so simple. It begs to be translated. And it has. No Zen text has been translated more. I would be surprised if there weren't a dozen versions in English alone. Normally, I wouldn't consider adding to an already crowded field. But whenever I've read the text, I've wanted to combine the couplets differently, differently from how I did the previous time I read the text or differently from how others combined them. The reason for this is that the Hsinhsinming is made up of rhymed couplets that don't necessarily rhyme anymore. The pronunciation of Chinese has changed. Hence, reading the text today, it's unclear which couplets go with which couplets. Are they quatrains or something else?

Fortunately, sometime between 584 and 589, a man named Lu Te-ming 陸德明 put together a book he called Exegesis of the Language of the Classics 經典釋文 (Ching-tien Shih-wen). This was a dictionary, and for each character Lu listed, he added two more to

---

6 Readers can judge for themselves. A PDF of Henrik Sorenson's English translation of the *Hsinming* is available online under the title "Mind Inscription."

indicate the pronunciation of both the initial and the final sound—all Chinese characters being mono-syllabic. A decade later, in 601, Lu Fa-yen 陸法言, published another book. He called it A Comparison of Rhymes 切韻 (Ch'ieh-yun). His goal was to provide poets at a loss for a rhyme with a convenient way to find something appropriate, and so he organized his book according to the way characters were pronounced. Using these two books and their successors, as well as inscriptions and other materials that have since come to light, scholars such as Bernard Karlgren[7] and, more recently, Baxter and Sagart[8] have reconstructed how Chinese was pronounced around 600—at least in the capitals of Ch'ang-an 長安 and Loyang 洛陽 where most of the material originated. Based on their work, we can see that the couplets that comprise the Hsinhsinming not only form standard two-couplet quatrains, they also form longer stanzas of three, four, six, and even eight couplets, and there is no longer a single couplet at the end in search of a rhyming pair, which had always puzzled me—and no doubt others.

In the pages that follow, I've presented the original Chinese text together with the T'ang pronunciation of the rhyme words. In my translations I've also indicated in bold the first line for each set of rhymes. It's still a single, continuous poem with a singular focus, but the different rhymes suggest, if nothing else, that it wasn't composed at one go but over time and with

---

7 Bernard Karlgren, *Grammata Serica Recensa* (1957).
8 William Baxter & Laurent Sagart, *Old Chinese Reconstruction, Version 1.1* (2014).

shifts of emphasis. After my line-by-line translation, I've also added a few notes, numbered according to which line they refer, but I've tried to keep them to a minimum and let the epigrams do the talking. Readers can find the entire poem sans interruptions at the very end of this chapbook. If it somehow approaches the epigrammatic style of the Chinese, it is in large part thanks to the help of Isaac Gardiner, who commented on seventeen different drafts.

As for the poem's meaning, it means about as much as any Zen text. In short, it doesn't mean. It isn't a finger pointing to the moon. If Seng-ts'an were alive, I can imagine him saying, "Where do you get this finger-moon business?" Seng-ts'an's poem is about non-duality. I remember when I first encountered this odd, cumbersome word. It was the Fall of 1972. I had dropped out of graduate school a few months earlier and had just arrived at the Buddhist monastery in southern Taiwan known as Fokuangshan 佛光山 (Buddha Light Mountain). The young monk who was showing me around my new home was Hsin-ting 心定.

One of the questions I asked was about the wording above the monastery's main gate. Written across the top were the characters 不二門, the Gate of Non-duality. What did that have to do with Buddhism, I wondered? Hsin-ting said that was the heart of Buddhism. I must have missed that page in the books I had been reading. I asked again, "If Buddhism means 'not two,' why not just say 'one,' why not the Gate of Oneness?" Hsin-ting said, "No, 'not two' doesn't mean 'one.' 'One' would only give rise to 'not one,' and we would have 'two' again. So we say, 'not two' and stop there." And as far as I can tell, that is what this poem is about.

Red Pine
Port Townsend
Spring 2019

Trusting the Mind

信
心
銘

Zen Epigrams

1. 至道無難／唯嫌揀擇 **draek**

2. 但莫憎愛／洞然明白 baek

3. 毫釐有差／天地縣隔 keak

4. 欲得現前／莫存順逆 gjaek

5. 違順相爭／是為心病 **bjaeng**

6. 不識玄旨／徒勞念靜 dzjeng

7. 圓同太虛／無欠無餘 **yo**

8. 良由取捨／所以不如 nyo

1. **The Way isn't hard to find**
   just avoid choosing
2. when preferences are gone
   it's perfectly clear
3. the slightest distinction
   parts heaven and earth
4. to find it right now
   don't take sides.
5. **Fighting over sides**
   is an illness of the mind
6. until you understand the mystery
   you still your thoughts in vain.
7. **It's perfect like the Void**
   there's nothing missing nothing extra
8. because you keep and throw away
   it doesn't look like that to you.

9. 莫逐有緣／勿住空忍 **nyin**

10. 一種平懷／泯然自盡 tsin

11. 止動歸止／止更彌動 **duwng**

12. 唯滯兩邊／寧知一種 tsyowng

13. 一種不通／兩處失功 kuwng

14. 遣有沒有／從空背空 khuwng

15. 多言多慮／轉不相應 ing

16. 絕言絕慮／無處不通 thuwng

9. **Don't chase dependent things**
   don't settle for emptiness either
10. in all-embracing oneness
    everything disappears completely.
11. **Staying still and trying not to move**
    you end up moving more
12. why be trapped in dualities
    realize opposites are the same
13. not knowing they're the same
    with either one you waste your time
14. denying existence or non-existence
    you trade one emptiness for another
15. the more you talk or think
    the more you don't make sense
16. when you stop talking and thinking
    there's nothing that isn't clear

17. 歸根得旨／隨照失宗 tsowng

18. 須臾返照／勝卻前空 khuwng

19. 前空轉變／皆由妄見 **ken**

20. 不用求真／唯須息見 ken

21. 二見不住／慎勿追尋 **xim**

22. 纔有是非／紛然失心 sim

23. 二由一有／一亦莫守 **syuw**

24. 一心不生／萬法無咎 gjuw

17. returning to the root you find the meaning
    following the light you end up confused
18. reflecting on this right now
    is better than before time began.
19. **Everything since time began**
    comes from deluded views
20. no need to look for the truth
    just put an end to views.
21. **Don't cling to dualities**
    and don't seek them out
22. once a yes or no appears
    confusion clouds the mind.
23. **Two exist because of one**
    let one go as well
24. when you don't think a single thought
    nothing is wrong with anything.

25. 無咎無法／不生不心 **sim**

26. 能隨境滅／境逐能沉 syim

27. 境由能境／能由境能 **noj**[6]

28. 欲知兩段／元是一空 khuwng

29. 一空同兩／齊含萬象 zjang

30. 不見精麤／寧有偏黨 tang

31. 大道體寬／無易無難 **nan**

32. 小見孤疑／轉急轉遲 drij[7]

---

6 The rhyme word 能 was pronounced *noj* in the twin capitals of the T'ang. Nowadays, it's pronounced as the velar nasal *neng*. My guess is that the author pronounced it *nung*.

7 Apparently someone decided to improve this line by replacing what was probably 懶 *lan*, meaning "slow" or "lazy"—and which rhymes with 難 *nan*—with 遲 *drij*, meaning "slow" or "tardy." The change makes better sense but at the expense of the rhyme.

25. **Nothing wrong and no things**
    no thought and no thinking
26. the actor disappears with the stage
    the stage disappears with the actor.
27. **The stage exists because of the actor**
    the actor exists because of the stage
28. realize these two things
    originally are one emptiness
29. one emptiness containing two
    altogether ten thousand things
30. if you don't distinguish fine or coarse
    how can you be one-sided?
31. **The Way at heart is all-embracing**
    it isn't hard or easy
32. those with doubts or narrow minds
    take longer the more they try.

33. 執之失度／必入邪路 **lu**

34. 放之自然／體無去住 drju

35. 任性合道／逍遙絕惱 **naw**

36. 繫念乖真／昏沉不好 xaw

37. 不好勞神／何用疏親 **tshin**

38. 欲取一乘／勿惡六塵 drin

39. 六塵不惡／還同正覺 **kaewk**

40. 智者無為／愚人自縛 bjak

33. **Grab it and you lose perspective**
    you're sure to go astray
34. let it be the way it is
    it doesn't leave or stay.
35. **Accept your nature be one with the Way**
    you'll know no discontent
36. control your thoughts oppose the truth
    you'll sink into negativity.
37. **Exhausting yourself in negativity**
    what use is leaving home
38. those who take the Path of Oneness
    give the dust of sensation no thought.
39. **Giving the dust of sensation no thought**
    this is the same as enlightenment
40. the wise do nothing
    fools become entangled

41. 法無異法／妄自愛著 drjak

42. 將心用心／豈非大錯 tshak

43. 迷生寂亂／悟無好惡 ak

44. 一切二邊／良由斟酌 tsyak

45. 夢幻空花／何勞把捉 tsraewk

46. 得失是非／一時放卻 khjak

47. 眼若不睡／諸夢自除 **dryo**

48. 心若不異／萬法一如 nyo

41. nothing differs from anything else
    but deluded people love attachments
42. they objectify the mind to cultivate the mind
    what a great mistake
43. peace and disorder arise from delusion
    enlightenment includes neither bad nor good
44. each and every duality
    is due to measures or scales
45. why bother trying to grab
    a dream an illusion a flower in the sky
46. profit and loss right and wrong
    let them go right now.
47. **When you're no longer asleep**
    dreams vanish by themselves
48. when you don't differentiate
    everything is real.

49. 一如體玄／兀爾忘緣 **ywen**

50. 萬法齊觀／歸復自然 nyen

51. 泯其所以／不可方比 **pjij**

52. 止動無動／動止無止 tsyi

53. 兩既不成／一何有爾 nej

54. 究竟窮極／不存軌則 **tsok**

55. 契心平等／所作俱息 sik

56. 孤疑淨盡／正信調直 drik

49. **What's real at heart is a mystery**
    be quiet and forget about reasons
50. view everything as one
    return to letting things be.
51. **When causes are gone**
    what is there to compare
52. be still and movement ceases
    move and stillness ends
53. if two things can't exist
    how can there be one?
54. **Go beyond all limits**
    don't follow patterns or rules
55. focus on equanimity
    stop whatever you're doing
56. get rid of lingering doubts
    put your trust in samadhi

57. 一切不留／無可記憶 ik

58. 虛明自照／不勞心力 lik

59. 非思量處／識情難測 tsrhik

60. 真如法界／無他無自 **dzij**

61. 要急相應／惟言不二 nyij

62. 不二皆同／無不包容 **yowng**

63. 十方智者／皆入此宗 tsowng

64. 宗非促延／一念萬年 **nen**

65. 無在不在／十方目前 dzen

57. let nothing at all remain
    nothing that leaves a trace
58. let the empty light shine
    don't exert your mind
59. this isn't the domain of reason
    much less perception or feeling.
60. **In the Dharma Realm of Suchness**
    neither self nor other exists
61. if you're ready right now
    just say "not two."
62. **Not two is all-inclusive**
    there's nothing it doesn't contain
63. the sages of every world
    all reach this understanding.
64. **An understanding that transcends time**
    a thought that lasts ten thousand years
65. there's nowhere it isn't present
    wherever you look it's there.

66. 極小同大／忘絕境界 **keaj**[6]

67. 極大同小／不見邊表 pjew

68. 有即是無／無即是有 hyuw

69. 若不如此／必不須守 syuw

70. 一即一切／一切即一 **jit**

71. 但能如是／何慮不畢 pjit

72. 信心不二／不二信心 **sim**

73. 言語道斷／非去來今 kim

---

6 A half rhyme suggesting the author spoke a dialect other than the one used in the capitals.

66. **It's smaller than small and bigger than big**
    forget about dimensions or states
67. it's bigger than big and smaller than small
    don't look for boundaries or edges
68. It exists but doesn't
    it doesn't but does
69. if this weren't true
    it wouldn't be worth your time.
70. **It's one and all things**
    it's all things and one
71. if you can be like this
    why care you're not done.
72. **Trust the mind free of dualities**
    free of dualities trust the mind
73. it's where language can't go
    it's not past future or present.

Notes

1. The Way 道. Chinese Buddhists felt so comfortable using the word *Tao*, or Way, they often preferred it to the Buddhist term *Dharma*. In fact, when Buddhism first arrived, the Chinese thought the Dharma was just a different kind of Taoism. Most commentators interpret 至 in the expression 至道 as an adjective ("ultimate"), citing Chuangtzu 莊子 (11.4), where the sage Kuang Ch'eng-tzu 廣成子 tells Huang-ti 黃帝 (the Yellow Emperor), "Come, I will tell you about the Ultimate Way. The heart of the Ultimate Way is deep and mysterious, the extent of the Ultimate Way is dark and silent." 來。吾語女至道。 至道之精，窈窈冥冥。至道之極，昏昏默默. The primary meaning of 至, however, is to "reach" or "find," and this seems to me to make better sense here, as well as better poetry.

6. Mystery 玄. Another term with a Taoist hue. Pronounced *hsuan*, it means "black with a drop of red in it" and is translated by "darkness" or "mystery." It's most famous use is in the first verse in Lao-tzu's *Taoteching* 道德經, where he defines the Tao as "the mystery beyond mysteries, the door to all beginnings" 玄之又玄 / 種眇之門. Taoism was sometimes called *Hsuanchiao* 玄教, "the teaching of mystery."

7. Void 太虛 or *T'ai-hsu*. This term was used to refer to the Taoist conception of non-duality. It was depicted as an empty circle and referred to the universe before it was divided into *yin* 陰 and *yang* 陽, heaven and earth.

9a. Dependent (or conditioned) things 有緣. Finally, a Buddhist term. According to the Buddhist point of view, things only exist in terms of their relation to other things. They have no self-existence and are inherently impermanent as well as empty.

9b. Emptiness 空. We say something exists. But because it doesn't exist by itself, we say it is empty of self-existence. When Buddhists use the word "emptiness," it is shorthand for this: "empty of self-existence." Seng-ts'an's concern is that such an insight is likely to become another form of attachment. Hence, he urges seeing emptiness not as a negative but as a positive, as he does in the next couplet.

10. Oneness 一種. Seng-ts'an's poem is a paean to non-duality, but at the same time it also advocates the doctrine of Oneness as presented in the *Lotus Sutra* 蓮華經, whereby not only is dependent existence to be transcended but emptiness as well.

11. Trying not to move 止動. Seng-ts'an is concerned that those who meditate might become attached to viewing meditation as stillness and trapped in yet another duality.

14. Existence or non-existence 有沒有. Deluded people think things are real, when in fact they only exist in relationship to other things. When the things they depend on are absent, they cease to exist. Thus we can

say they don't exist. But what about the idea that they exist, doesn't that exist? Hence, we can also say that they don't not exist—a negation of a negation. And so we're back where we began.

18. Before time began 前空. A literal translation would be "before the last empty (kalpa)." Buddhists appropriated the early Indian conception of cyclical time as divided into four kalpas, or phases, the last of which is an empty kalpa and after which a new kalpa begins. This expression became an early subject of meditation among Zen masters: "Who were you before the last empty kalpa?" 空劫以前自己. I can't help wonder if this wasn't its origin, at least as far as recorded uses go.

29. One emptiness containing two, altogether ten thousand things 一空同兩 , 齊含萬象. The Taoist conception of creation, as stated in Lao-tzu's *Taoteching* (42), is similar: "One gives birth to two (yin and yang), two give birth to three (yin, yang, and the mixture of the two), three give birth to the ten thousand things."

37. Leaving home 疎親. Literally, "distancing oneself from loved ones," in short, becoming a monk or nun or any spiritual wanderer.

38. Path of Oneness 一乘 (Sanskrit: *ekayana*). This refers to the Buddha's teaching in such sutras as the *Lotus* that emphasize one path, one mind, etc., as opposed to

multiple paths or minds. The Tientai school of Chinese Buddhism was founded on such doctrines by Seng-ts'an's contemporary Chih-yi 智顗 (538-597), the school's First Patriarch. The school's Third Patriarch, Chan-jan 湛然 (711-782), was one of Seng-ts'an's greatest admirers.

40a. Do nothing 無為. This is one of Taoism's most famous expressions: *wu-wei*, where *wei* 為 means to "do" or "fabricate," and wu means "no" or "nothing."

40b. Become entangled 自縛. The Chinese character 縛 *fu* is used by Chinese Buddhists to translate the Sanskrit *bandhana*, meaning "rope" or "to tie," and refers to the Three Entanglements of attraction, repulsion, and ignorance.

42. Objectify the mind 將心 to cultivate the mind 用心. This is aimed at those who see cultivation as consisting in turning the mind into an object, whereby awareness is viewed as looking into a mirror.

45. Flower in the sky 空中花. A common metaphor for the illusoriness of what we think of as real. Its origin was as a reference to cataracts.

48 & 49. Real 一如. Another Buddhist term (Sanskrit: *bhutatathata*), this refers to what is free of distinctions of space, time, or conception. It is sometimes described as the ocean as opposed to the waves.

56. Samadhi 調直. This Chinese compound was used as an early definition of the Sanskrit word *samadhi*: the state of absorption of mind and object. The three couplets that follow describe what is meant.

58. Empty light 虛明. This term refers to the mind free of delusions, a cloudless sky, and sensation separate from the skandhas of form, perception, memory, and consciousness.

60. Dharma Realm of Suchness 真如界. What is ultimately or intrinsically real. In texts where the words *Tao* and *Dharma* are both used, Tao (road) emphasizes reality as process, while Dharma (from *dhri*: to grasp) emphasizes reality as conception, not that there is any difference.

71. Not done 不畢. Enlightenment doesn't mean you've reached the end of the Path. What about all those beings you vowed to liberate? Have a cup of tea and get back to work.

72. Trust the mind 信心. Why not? What else is there?

Trusting the Mind

The Way isn't hard to find
just avoid choosing
when preferences are gone
it's perfectly clear
the slightest distinction
parts heaven and earth
to find it right now
don't take sides
fighting over sides
is an illness of the mind
until you understand the mystery
you still your thoughts in vain
it's perfect like the Void
there's nothing missing nothing extra
because you keep and throw away
it doesn't look like that to you
don't chase dependent things
don't settle for emptiness either
in all-embracing oneness
everything disappears completely
staying still and trying not to move
you end up moving more
why be trapped in dualities
realize opposites are the same
not knowing they're the same
with either one you waste your time

denying existence or non-existence
you trade one emptiness for another
the more you talk or think
the more you don't make sense
when you stop talking and thinking
there's nothing that isn't clear
returning to the root you find the meaning
following the light you end up confused
reflecting on this right now
is better than before time began
everything since time began
comes from deluded views
no need to look for the truth
just put an end to views
don't cling to dualities
and don't seek them out
once a yes or no appears
confusion clouds the mind
two exist because of one
let one go as well
when you don't think a single thought
nothing is wrong with anything
nothing wrong and no things
no thought and no thinking
the actor disappears with the stage
the stage disappears with the actor
the stage exists because of the actor
the actor exists because of the stage

realize these two things
originally are one emptiness
one emptiness containing two
altogether ten thousand things
if you don't distinguish fine or coarse
how can you be one-sided
the Way at heart is all-embracing
it isn't hard or easy
those with doubts or narrow minds
take longer the more they try
grab it and you lose perspective
you're sure to go astray
let it be the way it is
it doesn't leave or stay
accept your nature be one with the Way
you'll know no discontent
control your thoughts oppose the truth
you'll sink into negativity
exhausting yourself in negativity
what use is leaving home
those who take the Path of Oneness
give the dust of sensation no thought
giving the dust of sensation no thought
this is the same as enlightenment
the wise do nothing
fools become entangled
nothing differs from anything else

but deluded people love attachments
they objectify the mind to cultivate the mind
what a great mistake
peace and disorder arise from delusion
enlightenment includes neither bad nor good
each and every duality
is due to measures or scales
why bother trying to grab
a dream an illusion a flower in the sky
profit and loss right and wrong
let them go right now
when you're no longer asleep
dreams vanish by themselves
when you don't differentiate
everything is real
what's real at heart is a mystery
be quiet and forget about reasons
view everything as one
return to letting things be
when causes are gone
what is there to compare
be still and movement ceases
move and stillness ends
if two things can't exist
how can there be one
go beyond all limits
don't follow patterns or rules
focus on equanimity

stop whatever you're doing
get rid of lingering doubts
put your trust in samadhi
let nothing at all remain
nothing that leaves a trace
let the empty light shine
don't exert your mind
this isn't the domain of reason
much less perception or feeling
in the Dharma Realm of Suchness
neither self nor other exists
if you're ready right now
just say "not two"
not two is all-inclusive
there's nothing it doesn't contain
the sages of every world
all reach this understanding
an understanding that transcends time
a thought that lasts ten thousand years
there's nowhere it isn't present
wherever you look it's there
it's smaller than small and bigger than big
forget about dimensions or states
it's bigger than big and smaller than small
don't look for boundaries or edges
it exists but doesn't
it doesn't but does
if this weren't true

it wouldn't be worth your time
it's one and all things
it's all things and one
if you can be like this
why care you're not done
trust the mind free of dualities
free of dualities trust the mind
it's where language can't go
it's not past future or present